Puritan Evangelism
A Biblical Approach

Puritan Evangelism
A Biblical Approach

Joel R. Beeke

REFORMATION HERITAGE BOOKS
Grand Rapids, Michigan

© 1999, 2007 Joel R. Beeke

Published by
Reformation Heritage Books
2965 Leonard St., NE
Grand Rapids, MI 49525
616-977-0889 / Fax 616-285-3246
e-mail: orders@heritagebooks.org
website: www.heritagebooks.org

1st edition printings
1999, 2001, 2004

2nd edition printings
2007, 2010

Chinese edition, 2001
Korean edition, 2002
Portuguese edition, 2003

Library of Congress Cataloging-in-Publication Data

Beeke, Joel R., 1952-
  Puritan evangelism : a biblical approach / by Joel R. Beeke.
-- 2nd ed.
      p. cm.
  Includes bibliographical references.
  ISBN 978-1-60178-026-3 (pbk. : alk. paper)
  1. Puritans--Doctrines. 2. Preaching. 3. Evangelistic work.
I. Title.
  BX9323.B44 2007
  269'.20882859--dc22

                    2007036605

*For additional Reformed literature, both new and used,
request a free book list from Reformation Heritage Books
at the above address.*

With gratitude for

Bartel Elshout

my Puritan evangelist friend of four decades,
faithful colleague in the ministry,
and able Dutch translator

Contents

CHAPTER ONE

◆

Introduction: Puritan Evangelism Defined

A great Puritan evangelist, John Rogers, warned his congregation against neglecting Scripture by telling them what God might say: "I have trusted you so long with my Bible...it lies in [some] houses all covered with dust and cobwebs, you care not to listen to it. Do you use my Bible so? Well, you shall have my Bible no longer."

Rogers then picked up his Bible and started walking away from the pulpit. Then he stopped, fell on his knees, and took on the voice of the people, who pleaded, "Lord, whatever Thou dost to us, take not Thy Bible from us; kill our children, burn our houses, destroy our goods; only spare us Thy Bible, take not away Thy Bible."

"Say you so?" the minister replied, impersonating God. "Well, I will try you a while longer; and here is my Bible for you. I will see how you use it, whether you will search it more, love it more, observe it more, and live more according to it."

Thomas Goodwin was so moved by Rogers's dra-

matic presentation that when he left church he wept
upon his horse's neck for fifteen minutes before he
felt strong enough to mount it.[1]

John Calvin and his Puritan successors did not
lack evangelistic zeal, as some have claimed. David
Calhoun has defended Calvin's work as a teacher and
practitioner of evangelism.[2] Similarly, I will show
how the Puritans brought the gospel to others in a
thoroughly scriptural manner.[3] First, I will define

---

1. Allen C. Guelzo, "The Puritan Preaching Ministry in Old
and New England," *Journal of Christian Reconstruction* 6, 2
(1980):24-25.

2. David B. Calhoun, "John Calvin: Missionary Hero or
Missionary Failure?," *Presbyterion* 5, 1 (1979):16-33. Cf. Samuel
M. Zwemer, "Calvinism and the Missionary Enterprise," *Theology
Today* 7, 2 (1950):206-216; Johannes van den Berg, "Calvin's
Missionary Message," *Evangelical Quarterly* 22 (1950):174-87;
G. Baez-Camargo, "The Earliest Protestant Missionary Venture in
Latin America," *Church History* 21, 2 (1952):135-45; Johannes van
den Berg, "Calvin and Missions," in *John Calvin: Contemporary
Prophet,* ed. J.T. Hoogstra (Grand Rapids: Baker, 1959), pp. 167-
84; Charles Chaney, "The Missionary Dynamic in the Theology
of John Calvin," *Reformed Review* 17, 3 (1964):24-38; Philip
E. Hughes, "John Calvin: Director of Missions," and R. Pierce
Beaver, "The Genevan Mission to Brazil," in *The Heritage of John
Calvin,* ed. John H. Bratt (Grand Rapids: Eerdmans, 1973), pp.
40-73; W. Stanford Reid, "Calvin's Geneva: A Missionary Centre,"
Reformed Theological Review 42, 3 (1983):65-73; J. Douglas
MacMillan, "Calvin, Geneva, and Christian Mission," *Reformed
Theological Journal* 5 (1989):5-17.

3. The best sources for a Puritan theology of evangelism
and missions are Sidney H. Rooy, *The Theology of Missions in
the Puritan Tradition. A Study of Representative Puritans:
Richard Sibbes, Richard Baxter, John Eliot, Cotton Mather, and
Jonathan Edwards* (Laurel, Miss.: Audubon Press, 2006), and

what I mean by Puritan evangelism, then show that the Puritan evangelistic message, based on Scripture, was doctrinal, practical, experimental, and symmetrical. Then I will examine the primary methods Puritans used to communicate the gospel—a plain style of preaching and the practice of catechetical evangelism. Finally, we will see that the Puritans believed that the message and methods of evangelism were inseparable from the inward disposition of an evangelist. That disposition included a heartfelt dependence on the Holy Spirit and earnest prayer that God's Word and Spirit would bless all evangelistic efforts.

A look at the scriptural message, methods, and disposition of Puritan evangelism should convict us of our need to return to a scriptural foundation for all

James I. Packer, *A Quest for Godliness: The Puritan Vision of the Christian Life* (Wheaton, Ill.: Crossway, 1990), chps. 2, 10, 17-19. Cf. Francis G. James, "Puritan Missionary Endeavors in Early New England" (M.A. thesis, Yale, 1938); Ernst Benz, "Pietist and Puritan Sources of Early Protestant World Missions," *Church History* 20, 2 (1951):28-55; Johannes van den Berg, *Constrained by Jesus' Love: An Inquiry into the Motives of the Missionary Awakening in Great Britain in the Period Between 1698 and 1815* (Kampen: J.H. Kok, 1956); Alden T. Vaughan, *New England Frontier: Puritan and Indian, 1620-1675* (Boston: Little, Brown and Company, 1965); R. Pierce Beaver, *Pioneers in Mission* (Grand Rapids: Eerdmans, 1966); Charles L. Chaney, *The Birth of Missions in America* (South Pasadena, Calif.: William Carey Library, 1976); William S. Barker, "The Rediscovery of the Gospel: The Reformation, the Westminster Divines, and Missions," *Presbyterion* 24, 1 (1998):38-45.

evangelism. As the Puritans adopted biblical principles of evangelism and became practitioners of them
in their ministries, so we should embody these same
principles in our teaching and work. We have much
to learn from the Puritans about how to evangelize.

In this brief study, our use of the word *Puritan*
includes not only those people who were ejected
from the Church of England by the Act of Uniformity
in 1662, but also those in Britain and North America
who, for several generations after the Reformation,
worked to reform and purify the church and to lead
people toward biblical, godly living, consistent with
the Reformed doctrines of grace.[4] Puritanism grew

---

4. Richard Mitchell Hawkes, "The Logic of Assurance in
English Puritan Theology," *Westminster Theological Journal*
52 (1990): 247. For the difficulties in, and attempts at, defining
Puritanism, see Ralph Bronkema, *The Essence of Puritanism*
(Goes: Oosterbaan and LeCointre, 1929); Leonard J. Trinterud,
"The Origins of Puritanism," *Church History* 20 (1951):37-57;
Jerald C. Brauer, "Reflections on the Nature of English Puritanism,"
Church History 23 (1954):98-109; Basil Hall, "Puritanism: The
Problem of Definition," in G. J. Cumming, ed., *Studies in Church
History*, vol. 2 (London: Nelson, 1965), pp. 283-96; Charles
H. George, "Puritanism as History and Historiography," *Past
and Present* 41 (1968):77-104; William Lamont, "Puritanism
as History and Historiography: Some Further Thoughts," *Past
and Present* 42 (1969):133-46; Richard Greaves, "The Nature
of the Puritan Tradition," in R. Buick Knox, ed., *Reformation,
Conformity and Dissent: Essays in Honour of Geoffrey Nuttall*
(London: Epworth Press, 1977), pp. 255-73; D.M. Lloyd-Jones,
"Puritanism and Its Origins," *The Puritans: Their Origins and
Successors* (Edinburgh: Banner of Truth Trust, 1987), pp. 237-59;
Packer, "Why We Need the Puritans," in *A Quest for Godliness*, pp.
21-36; Joel R. Beeke, *The Quest for Full Assurance: The Legacy*

out of at least three needs: (1) the need for biblical preaching and the teaching of sound, Reformed doctrine; (2) the need for biblical, personal piety that stresses the work of the Holy Spirit in the faith and life of the believer; and (3) the need for a restoration of biblical simplicity in liturgy, vestments, and church government, so that a well-ordered church life would promote the worship of the triune God as prescribed in His Word.[5] Doctrinally, Puritanism was a kind of broad and vigorous Calvinism; experientially, it was a warm and contagious kind of Christianity; evangelistically, it was tender as well as aggressive.[6]

"Evangelism" is not a word the Puritans commonly used, but they were evangelists nonetheless. Richard Baxter's *Call to the Unconverted* and Joseph Alleine's *Alarm to the Unconverted* were pioneer works in evangelistic literature. Evangelism was, for these and other Puritans, a Word-centered task of the church, particularly of her ministers. They understood well the centrality of preaching, the role of the pastor, and the necessity of prayer in evangelism. They were truly "fishers of men," seeking to awaken the unconverted to their need of Christ, to lead them

of Calvin and His Successors (Edinburgh: Banner of Truth Trust, 1999), pp. 82ff.

5. Peter Lewis, *The Genius of Puritanism* (Morgan, Pa.: Soli Deo Gloria, 1997), pp. 11ff.

6. Rooy, *Theology of Missions in the Puritan Tradition*, pp. 310-28.

to faith and repentance, and to establish them in a lifestyle of sanctification.

The expression "Puritan evangelism," then, refers to how the Puritans proclaimed what God's Word counsels regarding the salvation of sinners from sin and its consequences. That salvation is granted by grace, received by faith, grounded in Christ, and reflective of the glory of God. For the Puritans, evangelism not only involved presenting Christ so that by the power of the Spirit people come to God through Him; it equally involved so presenting Christ that the believer may grow in Him, and serve Him as Lord in the fellowship of His church and in the extension of His kingdom in the world. Puritan evangelism involved declaring the entire economy of redemption by focusing on the saving work of all three Persons of the Trinity, while simultaneously calling sinners to a life of fath and commitment, and warning that the gospel will condemn forever those who persist in unbelief and impenitence.[7]

---

7. *The Complete Works of Thomas Manton*, ed. T. Smith. (1870; reprint Worthington, Pa.: Maranatha, 1980), 2:102ff.

Characteristics of
Puritan Preaching

CHAPTER TWO

———————— ♦ ————————

Thoroughly Biblical

In discussing the message of Puritan evangelism, we will focus on five distinctive characteristics of Puritan preaching and consider how those characteristics differ from what is used in evangelistic preaching today.

First, then, Puritan preaching was *thoroughly biblical.* The Puritan preacher found his message in God's Word. "The faithfull Minister, like unto Christ, [is] one that preacheth nothing but the word of God," said Puritan Edward Dering.[1] John Owen agreed: "The first and principal duty of a pastor is to feed the flock by diligent preaching of the word."[2] As Miller Maclure noted, "For the Puritans, the sermon is not just hinged to Scripture; it quite literally exists inside the Word of God; the text is not in the sermon, but

———————————

1. *M. Derings Workes* (1597; reprint New York: Da Capo Press, 1972), p. 456.

2. *The Works of John Owen*, ed. William H. Goold (1853; reprint London: Banner of Truth Trust, 1965), 16:74.

the sermon is in the text.... Put summarily, listening to a sermon is being in the Bible."[3]

The Puritans were people of the living Book. They loved, lived, and breathed Scripture, relishing the power of the Spirit that accompanied the Word.[4] They regarded the sixty-six books of Scripture as the library of the Holy Spirit that was graciously bequeathed to them. They viewed Scripture as God speaking to them as a father speaks to his children. They saw the Word as truth they could trust in and rest upon for all eternity. They saw it empowered by the Spirit to renew their minds and transform their lives.

The Puritans searched, heard, and sang the Word with delight, and encouraged others to do the same. Puritan Richard Greenham suggested eight ways to read Scripture: with diligence, wisdom, preparation, meditation, conference, faith, practice, and prayer.[5]

---

3. *The Paul's Cross Sermons, 1534-1642* (Toronto: University of Toronto Press, 1958), p. 165.

4. See Joel R. Beeke and Ray B. Lanning, "The Transforming Power of Scripture," in *Sola Scriptura: The Protestant Position of the Bible*, ed. Don Kistler (Morgan, Pa.: Soli Deo Gloria, 1995), pp. 221-76.

5. "A Profitable Treatise, Containing a Direction for the reading and understanding of the holy Scriptures," in H[enry] H[olland], ed., *The Works of the Reverend and Faithfvll Servant of Iesvs Christ, M. Richard Greenham* (1599; reprint New York: Da Capo Press, 1973), pp. 389-97. Cf. Thomas Watson, "How We May Read the Scriptures with Most Spiritual Profit," in *Heaven Taken by Storm: Showing the Holy Violence a Christian is to Put Forth in the Pursuit After Glory*, ed. Joel R. Beeke (1669; reprint Pittsburgh: Soli Deo Gloria, 1992), pp. 113-129.

Thomas Watson provided numerous guidelines on how to listen to the Word. Come to the Word with a holy appetite and a teachable heart. Sit under the Word attentively, receive it with meekness, and mingle it with faith. Then retain the Word, pray over it, practice it, and speak to others about it.[6] "Dreadful is their case who go loaded with sermons to hell," Watson warned. By contrast, those who respond to Scripture as a "love letter sent to you from God" will experience its warming, transforming power.[7]

"Feed upon the Word," the Puritan preacher John Cotton exhorted his congregation.[8] The preface to the Geneva Bible contains similar advice, saying the Bible is "the light to our paths, the key of the kingdom of heaven, our comfort in affliction, our shield and sword against Satan, the school of all wisdom, the glass wherein we behold God's face, the testimony of his favor, and the only food and nourishment of our souls."[9]

The Puritans sounded a clarion call to become

---

6. Ibid., pp. 16-18, and Thomas Watson, *A Body of Divinity* (1692; reprint London: Banner of Truth Trust), pp. 377-79.

7. Ibid., p. 379. "There is not a sermon which is heard, but it sets us nearer heaven or hell" (John Preston, *A Pattern of Wholesome Words,* quoted in Christopher Hill, *Society and Puritanism in Pre-Revolutionary England,* 2nd ed. (New York: Schocken, 1967), p. 46.

8. *Christ the Fountain of Life* (London: Carden, 1648), p. 14.

9. *Geneva Bible* (1599; reprint Ozark, Mo.: L.L. Brown, 1990), p. 3.

intensely Word-centered in faith and practice. They regarded the Bible as a trustworthy guide for all of life. "We should set the Word of God alway before us like a rule, and believe nothing but that which it teacheth, love nothing but that which it prescribeth, hate nothing but that which it forbiddeth, do nothing but that which it commandeth," said the Puritan preacher Henry Smith to his congregation.[10] "The Scriptures teach us the best way of living, the noblest way of suffering, and the most comfortable way of dying," wrote John Flavel.

No wonder, then, that a typical page of a Puritan evangelistic sermon contains five to ten citations of biblical texts and about a dozen references to texts. Puritan preachers were conversant with their Bibles; they memorized hundreds, if not thousands, of texts. They knew what Scripture to cite for any concern. "Long and personal familiarity with the application of Scripture was a key element in the Puritan ministerial makeup," Sinclair Ferguson writes. "They pondered the riches of revealed truth the way a gemologist patiently examines the many faces of a diamond."[11] They used Scripture wisely, bringing cited texts to

---

10. "Food for New-Born Babes," in *The Works of Henry Smith,* ed. Thomas Smith (1866; reprint Stoke-on-Trent, UK: Tentmaker Publications, 2002), 1:494.

11. "Evangelical Ministry: The Puritan Contribution," in *The Compromised Church: The Present Evangelical Crisis,* ed. John H. Armstrong (Wheaton, Ill.: Crossway, 1998), p. 267.

bear on the doctrine or case of conscience[12] at hand, all based on sound hermeneutical principles.[13]

The evangelistic sermons of contemporary preachers often incorporate verses wrested out of context or a string of texts that do not belong together. Modern evangelism, in quest of a "simple gospel," favors a mere formula, a packaged presentation, instead of the whole counsel of God. Moreover, some preachers seem to have a better understanding of professional football and television programs, or of the teachings of Sigmund Freud and Paul Tillich, than they do of Moses and Paul.

Puritan preachers, for the most part, were well-grounded in biblical languages and classical learning. But they were also men who were convinced of the need to be "born again, not of corruptible seed, but of incorruptible, by the word of God, which liveth and abideth for ever" (1 Pet. 1:23). They were persuaded that the Holy Spirit worked through Scripture to bring truth home to sinners. The very thought

12. E.g., *William Perkins, 1558-1602: English Puritanist. His Pioneer Works on Casuistry: "A Discourse of Conscience" and "The Whole Treatise of Cases of Conscience,"* ed. Thomas F. Merrill (Nieuwkoop: B. DeGraaf, 1966). These works earned Perkins the title of "the father of Puritan casuistry."

13. See Packer, *A Quest for Godliness,* pp. 81-106; Leland Ryken, *Worldly Saints: The Puritans as They Really Were* (Grand Rapids: Zondervan, 1986), pp. 143-49, 154; Thomas D. Lea, "The Hermeneutics of the Puritans," *Journal of the Evangelical Theological Society* 39, 2 (1996):271-84.

patterns of the Puritans were steeped in the exact phraseology of the Bible.

If we are ever prone to be proud of our Bible knowledge, we ought to open any volume of John Owen, Thomas Goodwin, or Thomas Brooks, note how some obscure passage in Nahum is quoted followed by a familiar passage from John—both of which perfectly illustrate the point the writer is making—then compare our knowledge to theirs. How can we explain this marvelous—for us, humbling—grasp of Scripture other than that these divines *were ministers of the Word?* These men obviously studied their Bibles daily, falling to their knees as God's Spirit burned the Word into their pastoral hearts. Then, as they wrote or preached their evangelistic messages, one scriptural passage after another would come to mind.

Our evangelistic efforts must be similarly grounded in the Bible. We must search the Scriptures more frequently and love the Word of God more fervently. As we learn to think, speak, and act more biblically, our messages will become more authoritative and our witness will become more effective and fruitful.

CHAPTER THREE

Unashamedly Doctrinal

Puritan preaching was *unashamedly doctrinal.* The Puritan evangelist saw theology as an essentially practical discipline. William Perkins called it "the science of living blessedly for ever";[1] William Ames, "the doctrine or teaching of living to God."[2] As Ferguson writes, "To them, systematic theology was to the pastor what a knowledge of anatomy is to the physician. Only in the light of the whole body of divinity (as they liked to call it) could a minister provide a diagnosis of, prescribe for, and ultimately cure spiritual disease in those who were plagued by the body of sin and death."[3]

The Puritans, therefore, were not afraid to preach the whole counsel of God. They did not conciliate their hearers by lightening up their messages with

---

1. *The Works of William Perkins* (London: John Legate, 1609), 1:10.

2. William Ames, *The Marrow of Theology,* ed. John D. Eusden (1629; Grand Rapids: Baker, 1997), p. 77.

3. *Compromised Church,* p. 266.

humorous stories or folksy anecdotes. They felt the awesome responsibility of handling eternal truth and addressing immortal souls (Ezek. 33:8). They preached the weighty truths of God,

> *As a dying man to dying men,*
> *As never sure to preach again!*

For example, when the Puritans dealt with the doctrine of sin, they called sin *sin*, and declared it to be moral rebellion against God which reaps eternal guilt. They preached about sins of commission and sins of omission in thought, word, and deed. Works such as Jeremiah Burroughs's *The Evil of Evils: The Exceeding Sinfulness of Sin,* stress the heinousness of sin. In sixty-seven chapters, Burroughs exposes sin for what it is: the least sin involves more evil than the greatest affliction; sin and God are contrary to each other; sin opposes all that is good; sin is the poison of all evils; sin bears an infinite dimension and character; and sin makes us comfortable with the devil.[4]

The Puritans linked sin with the fall of Adam and Eve in Paradise.[5] They taught in no uncertain

---

4. Burroughs, *The Evil of Evils* (1654; reprint Morgan, Pa.: Soli Deo Gloria, 1995). Cf. Ralph Venning, *The Plague of Plagues* (1669; reprint London: Banner of Truth Trust, 1965); Thomas Watson, *The Mischief of Sin* (1671; reprint, Morgan, Pa.: Soli Deo Gloria, 1994); Samuel Bolton, "Sin: the Greatest Evil," in *Puritans on Conversion* (Pittsburgh: Soli Deo Gloria, 1990), pp. 1-69.

5. The most powerful Puritan work on the dread consequences of original sin is Thomas Goodwin, "An Unregenerate Man's Guiltiness Before God in Respect of Sin and Punishment," vol. 10

terms that through that fall we inherit the depravity that makes us unfit for God, holiness, and heaven. "In Adam's fall, we sinnéd all," they affirmed. They stressed that the problem of sinners was twofold: a bad record, which is a legal problem; and a bad heart, which is a moral problem. Both make us unfit for communion with God. More than an outward reformation of life is needed to meet the demands of God; inward regeneration of heart through a triune God is essential for salvation (John 3:3-7).

The Puritans also preached the doctrine of God without equivocation. They proclaimed God's majestic being, His trinitarian personality, and His glorious attributes.[6] All of their evangelism was

of *The Works of Thomas Goodwin* (1865; reprint Grand Rapids: Reformation Heritage Books, 2006). The classic doctrinal Puritan work on the subject is Jonathan Edwards, *Original Sin,* vol. 3 of *The Works of Jonathan Edwards* (1758; New Haven: Yale, 1970). The best secondary source on the Edwardsean view is C. Samuel Storms, *Tragedy in Eden: Original Sin in the Theology of Jonathan Edwards* (Lanham, Md.: University Press of America, 1985). Thomas Boston's classic, *Human Nature in Its Fourfold State* (1720; reprint London: Banner of Truth Trust, 1964), focuses on the four states of innocence, depravity, grace, and glory, but his section on imputed and inherited depravity is especially poignant. He details how Adam's original sin broke man's relationship with God as well as each of the Ten Commandments.

6. The classic work on God's attributes is Stephen Charnock's massive *Discourses on the Existence and Attributes of God* (1682; reprint Grand Rapids: Baker, 1996). See also William Bates, *The Harmony of the Divine Attributes in the Contrivance and Accomplishment of Man's Redemption* (1674; reprint Harrisonburg, Va.: Sprinkle, 1985).

rooted in a robust biblical theism, unlike modern evangelism which too often approaches God as if He were a next-door neighbor who can adjust His attributes to our needs and desires. While modern evangelism claims John 3:16 as its text, the Puritan would more likely cite Genesis 1:1, "In the beginning God," to show how everything that happened since is part of what God has designed for His own glory. The Puritans understood that the doctrines of atonement, justification, and reconciliation are meaningless apart from a true understanding of God who condemns sin, and atones for sinners, justifies them, and reconciles them to Himself.

Puritan evangelism also proclaimed the doctrine of Christ. "Preaching is the chariot that carries Christ up and down the world," wrote Richard Sibbes.[7] In works such as Thomas Taylor's *Christ Revealed,* Thomas Goodwin's *Christ Our Mediator,* Alexander Grosse's *Happiness of Enjoying and Making a Speedy Use of Christ,* Isaac Ambrose's *Looking Unto Jesus,* Ralph Robinson's or Philip Henry's *Christ All in All,* John Brown's *Christ: the Way, the Truth, and the Life,* John Owen's *The Glorious Mystery of the Person of Christ,* and James Durham's *Christ Crucified,* the Puritans preached the whole Christ to the

---

7. *The Complete Works of Richard Sibbes,* ed. Alexander B. Grosart (1862; reprint Edinburgh: Banner of Truth Trust, 1977), 5:508.

whole man.[8] They offered Him as Prophet, Priest, and King. They did not separate His benefits from His person or offer Him as a Savior from sin while ignoring His claims as Lord. As Joseph Alleine wrote in his model of Puritan evangelism,[9] *An Alarm to the Unconverted:*

---

8. Thomas Taylor, *Christ Revealed: or The Old Testament Explained; A Treatise of the Types and Shadowes of our Saviour* (London: M.F. for R. Dawlman and L. Fawne, 1635) is the best Puritan work on Christ in the Old Testament. Thomas Goodwin, "Christ Our Mediator," vol. 5 of *The Works of Thomas Goodwin* ably expounds primary New Testament texts on the mediatorship of Christ. Alexander Grosse, *The Happiness of Enjoying and Making a Trve And Speedy use of Christ* (London: Tho: Brudenell, for John Bartlet, 1647) and Isaac Ambrose, *Looking Unto Jesus* (1658; reprint Harrisonburg, Va.: Sprinkle, 1988) are experiential Christology at its best. Ralph Robinson, *Christ All and In All: or Several Significant Similitudes by which the Lord Jesus Christ is Described in the Holy Scriptures* (1660; reprint Ligonier, Pa.: Soli Deo Gloria, 1992), Philip Henry, *Christ All in All, or What Christ is Made to Believers* (1676; reprint Swengel, Pa.: Reiner, 1976), and John Brown, *Christ: the Way, the Truth, and the Life* (1677; reprint Morgan, Pa.: Soli Deo Gloria, 1995) contain precious sermons extolling Christ in all His relations to believers. John Owen, *A Declaration of the Glorious Mystery of the Person of Christ* (1679; reprinted in vol. 1 of *Works of Owen*) is superb on the relation of Christ's natures to His person. James Durham, *Christ Crucified; or The Marrow of the Gospel in 72 Sermons on Isaiah 53* (1683; reprint Dallas: Naphtali Press, 2001) remains unrivaled as a scriptural exposition of Christ's passion.

9. Joseph Alleine, *An Alarm to the Unconverted* (1671; reprint London: Banner of Truth Trust, 1959), p. 11. This book was reprinted again by Banner of Truth Trust in 1995 as *A Sure Guide to Heaven,* a title first used in 1675.

> All of Christ is accepted by the sincere convert. He loves not only the wages but the work of Christ, not only the benefits but the burden of Christ. He is willing not only to tread out the corn, but to draw under the yoke. He takes up the commands of Christ, yea, the cross of Christ. The unsound convert takes Christ by halves. He is all for the salvation of Christ, but he is not for sanctification. He is for the privileges, but does not appropriate the person of Christ. He divides the offices and benefits of Christ. This is an error in the foundation. Whoever loves life, let him beware here. It is an undoing mistake, of which you have often been warned, and yet none is more common.[10]

Alleine shows us that the dividing of the offices and benefits of Christ is not a twentieth-century invention. Throughout the ages man has rebelled against Christ as God offers Him—as Savior and Lord (Ps. 2). The true convert, however, is willing to receive a whole Christ, without limitations. "He is willing to have Christ upon any terms; he is willing to have the dominion of Christ as well as deliverance by Christ," Alleine said.[11]

This unreserved receiving of Christ is especially evident in written covenants entered into by Puritans. Puritan preachers encouraged their listeners to "close with" (appropriate) a freely offered Christ by faith, then draft and sign a document of total commitment, in which they "covenanted" (surrendered)

---

10. Ibid., p. 45.
11. Ibid., pp. 45-46.

their entire lives to God. These moving covenants are found in numerous Puritan diaries and evangelistic books.[12] The Puritans would stand aghast at the present trend in modern evangelism which seeks merely to rescue sinners from hell, postponing their submission to the sovereign lordship of Christ until later.

Preaching Christ with winsomeness and grace was the greatest burden and most essential task of the Puritan evangelist. "Christ crucified" must be "the subject matter of gospel-preaching," Robert Traill said. "Two things ministers have to do:... 1. To set him forth to people; to paint him in his love, excellency, and ability to save. 2. To offer him unto them freely, fully, without any limitation as to sinners, or their sinful state."[13] Robert Bolton agreed: "Jesus Christ is offered most freely, and without exception of any person, every Sabbath, every Sermon."[14] The Puritan evangelists repeatedly presented Christ in His ability, willingness to save, and preciousness as

12. E.g., see ibid., pp. 117-20; William Guthrie, *The Christian's Great Interest* (1658; reprint London: Banner of Truth Trust, 1969), pp. 169-92; Richard Alleine, *Heaven Opened: The Riches of God's Covenant of Grace* (1666; Morgan, Pa.: Soli Deo Gloria, 2000); Philip Doddridge, *The Rise and Progress of Religion in the Soul* (1744; Edinburgh: for Ogle, Allardice, & Thomson, 1819), pp. 217-26.

13. "By what Means may Ministers best win Souls?," in *The Works of Robert Traill* (1810; Edinburgh: Banner of Truth Trust, 1975), 1:246.

14. *A Treatise on Comforting Afflicted Consciences* (1626; reprint Ligonier, Pa.: Soli Deo Gloria, 1991), p. 185.

the only Redeemer of lost sinners. They did so with theological articulation, divine grandeur, and human passion. They extolled Christ to the highest as both an objective and a subjective Savior, and abased man to the lowest. They were not worried about injuring the self-esteem of listeners. They were far more concerned about esteeming the triune God: the Father who created us with dignity in His image; the Son who restores that dignity to us through redemption and the adoption of sons; and the Holy Spirit who indwells us and makes our souls and bodies His temple. Self-esteem messages which do not center upon a triune God they would have viewed as "self-deceit" messages. We have nothing to esteem in ourselves apart from God, the Puritans said. Apart from His grace, we are fallen, wretched, unworthy, and hell-bound.

To mention only one more doctrine, Puritan evangelists also stressed sanctification.[15] The believer must walk the king's highway of holiness in grati-

---

15. The Puritan classic on sanctification is Walter Marshall, *The Gospel Mystery of Sanctification* (1692; reprint Grand Rapids: Reformation Heritage Books, 1999). Marshall effectively grounds the doctrine of sanctification in a believer's union with Christ and underscores the necessity of practical holiness in everyday living. See also Lewis Bayly, *The Practice of Piety* (1611; reprint Morgan, Pa.: Soli Deo Gloria, 1996); Henry Scudder, *The Christian's Daily Walk, in Holy Security and Peace,* 6th ed. (1635; reprint Harrisonburg, Va.: Sprinkle, 1984); Henry Scougal, *The Life of God in the Soul of Man* (1739; reprint Harrisonburg, Va.: Sprinkle, 1986).

tude, service, obedience, love, and self-denial.[16] He must know experientially the continued exercise of the twin graces of faith and repentance.[17] He must learn the art of meditation, of fearing God, and of childlike prayer.[18] He must press on by God's grace, seeking to make his calling and election sure.[19]

---

16. See Thomas Brooks, "The Crown and Glory of Christianity: or Holiness, The only way to Happiness," in *The Works of Thomas Brooks,* vol. 4 (1864; reprint Edinburgh: Banner of Truth Trust, 1980); George Downame, *The Christian's Freedom: The Doctrine of Christian Liberty* (1633; reprint Pittsburgh, Pa.: Soli Deo Gloria, 1994); Samuel Bolton, *The True Bounds of Christian Freedom* (1645; reprint London: Banner of Truth Trust, 1964); Jonathan Edwards, *Charity and Its Fruits* (1852; reprint London: Banner of Truth Trust, 1969); Thomas Watson, *The Duty of Self-Denial* (1675; Morgan, Pa.: Soli Deo Gloria, 1995), pp. 1-37.

17. See Samuel Ward, "The Life of Faith," in *Sermons and Treatises by Samuel Ward* (1636; Edinburgh: Banner of Truth Trust, 1996), pp. 15-40; Thomas Watson, *The Doctrine of Repentance* (1668; reprint Edinburgh: Banner of Truth Trust, 1987).

18. See Nathanael Ranew, *Solitude Improved by Divine Meditation* (1670; reprint Morgan, Pa.: Soli Deo Gloria, 1995); Jeremiah Burroughs, *Gospel Fear* (1647; reprint, Pittsburgh, Pa.: Soli Deo Gloria, 1991); Thomas Cobbet, *Gospel Incense, Or A Practical Treatise on Prayer* (1657; reprint Pittsburgh: Soli Deo Gloria, 1993); John Bunyan, *Prayer* (London: Banner of Truth Trust, 1965); John Preston, Nathaniel Vincent, Samuel Lee, *The Puritans on Prayer* (Morgan, Pa.: Soli Deo Gloria, 1995).

19. William Perkins, "A Christian and Plain Treatise on the Manner and Order of Predestination, and of the Largeness of God's Grace," in *Works*, 2:687-730; Anthony Burgess, *Spiritual Refining* (1652; Ames, Ia.: International Outreach, 1990), pp. 643-74.

CHAPTER FOUR

———— ◆ ————

Experimentally Practical

Puritan preaching was *experimentally practical*. Puritan preaching explained how a Christian experiences biblical truth in his life. The term *experimental* comes from the Latin word *experimentum*, which is derived from the verb which means to "try, test, prove, or put to the test." The same verb can also mean "to find or know by experience," and so gives rise to the word *experientia*, meaning "trial, experiment" and "the knowledge gained by experiment."[1] Calvin used experiential (*experientia*) and experimental (*experimentum*) interchangeably, since both words, from the perspective of biblical preaching, indicate the need for examining or testing experienced knowledge by the touchstone of Scripture (Isa. 8:20).[2]

---

1. *Cassell's Latin Dictionary,* revised J. R. V. Marchant and J. F. Charles (New York: Funk & Wagnalls, n.d.).

2. Willem Balke, "The Word of God and *Experientia* according to Calvin," in *Calvinus Ecclesiae Doctor,* ed. W. H. Neuser (Kampen: J.H. Kok, 1978), pp. 20-21; cf. Calvin's *Commentary* on Zechariah 2:9.

Experimental preaching stresses the need to know by experience the truths of the Word of God. Experimental preaching seeks to explain in terms of biblical truth, how matters *ought to go* and how they *do go* in the Christian life, and aims to apply divine truth to the whole range of the believer's experience: in his walk with God as well as his relationship with family, the church, and the world around him. We can learn much from the Puritans about this type of preaching. As Paul Helm writes:

> The situation calls for preaching that will cover the full range of Christian experience, and a developed experimental theology. The preaching must give guidance and instruction to Christians in terms of their actual experience. It must not deal in unrealities or treat congregations as if they lived in a different century or in wholly different circumstances. This involves taking the full measure of our modern situation and entering with full sympathy into the actual experiences, the hopes and fears, of Christian people.[3]

The experimental preaching of the Puritans focused on the preaching of Christ. As Scripture clearly shows, evangelism must bear witness to the record God has given of His only begotten Son (Acts 2:30-36; 5:42; 8:35; Rom. 16:25; 1 Cor. 2:2; Gal. 3:1). The Puritans thus taught that any preaching in which Christ does not have the preeminence is not valid

---

3. "Christian Experience," *Banner of Truth,* No. 139 (Apr. 1975):6.

experiential preaching. William Perkins said that the heart of all preaching was to "preach one Christ by Christ to the praise of Christ."[4] According to Thomas Adams, "Christ is the sum of the whole Bible, prophesied, typified, prefigured, exhibited, demonstrated, to be found in every leaf, almost in every line, the Scriptures being but as it were the swaddling bands of the child Jesus."[5] "Think of Christ as the very substance, marrow, soul, and scope of the whole Scriptures," Isaac Ambrose said.[6]

In this Christ-centered context, Puritan evangelism was marked by a discriminating application of truth to experience. Discriminatory preaching defines the difference between the non-Christian and the Christian. Discriminatory preaching pronounces the wrath of God and eternal condemnation upon the unbelieving and impenitent. It likewise offers the forgiveness of sins and eternal life to all who embrace by true faith Jesus Christ as Savior and Lord. Such preaching teaches that if our religion is not experiential, we will perish—not because experience itself saves, but because Christ who saves sinners must be experienced personally as the Rock upon whom our eternal hope is built (Matt. 7:22-27; 1 Cor. 1:30; 2:2).

---

4. *Works of Perkins,* 2:762.

5. *The Works of Thomas Adams* (1862; reprint Eureka, Calif.: Tanski, 1998), 3:224.

6. *Works of Isaac Ambrose* (London: for Thomas Tegg & Son, 1701), p. 201.

The Puritans were very aware of the deceitfulness of the human heart. Consequently, Puritan evangelists took great pains to identify the marks of grace that distinguish the church from the world, true believers from merely professing believers, and saving faith from temporary faith.[7] Thomas Shepard in *The Ten Virgins,* Matthew Mead in *The Almost Christian Discovered,* Jonathan Edwards in *Religious Affections,* and other Puritans wrote dozens of works to differentiate imposters from true believers.[8]

That kind of discriminatory preaching is extremely rare today. Even in conservative evangelical churches, head knowledge of scriptural truth is often a substitute for heart experience, or, what is equally unscriptural, heart experience is substituted for head knowledge. Experimental preaching calls for both head knowledge and heart experience; its goal, according to John Murray, is "intelligent piety." Experimental preaching is "Christianity brought home to men's business and bosoms," Robert Burns said. "The principle on which experimental religion

---

7. Thomas Watson, *The Godly Man's Picture* (1666; reprint Edinburgh: Banner of Truth Trust, 1992), pp. 20-188, sets forth twenty-four marks of grace for self-examination.

8. Thomas Shepard, *The Parable of the Ten Virgins* (1660; reprint Ligonier, Pa.: Soli Deo Gloria, 1990); Matthew Mead, *The Almost Christian Discovered; Or the False Professor Tried and Cast* (1662; reprint Ligonier, Pa.: Soli Deo Gloria, 1988); Jonathan Edwards, *Religious Affections* (New Haven: Yale University Press, 1959).

rests is simply this, that Christianity should not only be known, and understood, and believed, but also felt, and enjoyed, and practically applied."[9]

How different this is from most contemporary preaching! The Word of God is often preached today in a way that will never transform anyone because it never discriminates and never applies. Preaching is reduced to a lecture, a catering to the wishes and needs of people, or a form of experientialism removed from the foundation of Scripture. Such preaching fails to expound from Scripture what the Puritans called vital religion: how a sinner is stripped of all his own righteousness, driven to Christ alone for salvation, finds joy in obedience and reliance upon Christ, encounters the plague of indwelling sin, battles against backsliding, and gains the victory through Christ.[10]

When God's Word is preached experimentally, the Holy Spirit uses it to transform men, women, and nations. Such preaching transforms because it corresponds to the vital experience of the children of God (Rom. 5:1-11), clearly explains the marks of saving grace in the believer (Matt. 5:3-12; Gal. 5:22-23), proclaims the high calling of believers as the ser-

---

9. Introduction to *The Works of Thomas Halyburton* (London: Thomas Tegg, 1835), pp. xiv-xv.

10. Joel R. Beeke, *Jehovah Shepherding His Sheep* (Grand Rapids: Reformation Heritage Books, 1997), pp. 164-203, and *Backsliding: Disease and Cure* (Grand Rapids: Reformation Heritage Books, 1997), pp. 17-32.

vants of God in the world (Matt. 5:13-16), and shows
the eternal destination of believers and unbelievers
(Rev. 21:1-9).[11]

Space does not permit me to show how the various stages of spiritual experience are neglected in
today's preaching. Let's focus instead on only the first
step—*conviction of sin*.[12] If we consider those periods from the apostolic age onwards when the gospel
advanced with the greatest success in the world and
conversions have been multiplied, then ask what element was evident at those times that is lacking today,
the absence of conviction of sin must be noted first of
all. D. Martyn Lloyd-Jones rightly pointed out that
the greatest problem of the present day church is
that she is far too "healthy." The church shows little
consciousness of spiritual need or distress. As J.S.
Sinclair, a twentieth-century Free Presbyterian minister, writes:

> Today, the sense of sin is absent from many sup-
> posed *conversions*. This important change is now

---

11. See the *Heidelberg Catechism* for a Reformed confessional
statement that facilitates experimental preaching. This is
evidenced by (1) the Catechism's exposition of an outline (misery,
deliverance, and gratitude) that is true to the experience of
believers, (2) its application of most doctrines directly to the
believer's conscience and spiritual profit, and (3) its warm,
personal character in which the believer is regularly addressed in
the second person.

12. For this section on conviction of sin, I am indebted for
several thoughts to addresses given by Iain Murray, Donald
Macleod, and Albert Martin.

generally reduced to one category, decision for Christ. All that the convert is expected to say is that he believes in and intends to follow Christ. There is no word of conviction of sin, and ruin, and helplessness. A lost sinner, crying to the Lord for mercy and pardon and faith through Jesus Christ, and not ceasing until he is helped and saved from above, is not the newer Christian at his beginnings. He believes and decides by his own native ability with hardly a pang of conscience, and this is what is called conversion.[13]

In all periods of revival and spiritual prosperity, including the Puritan era, a sense of sin is common. In his preface to Jonathan Edwards's *A Narrative of Surprising Conversions,* Isaac Watts wrote, "Wheresoever God works with power for salvation upon the minds of men, there will be some discoveries of a sense of sin, of the danger of the wrath of God, and the all-sufficiency of His Son Jesus, to relieve us under all our spiritual wants and distresses, and a hearty consent of soul to receive him in the various offices of grace, wherein he is set forth in the Holy Scriptures."[14]

Genuine revivals are always accompanied by profound conviction of sin. That is due to the Holy Spirit, whose first work in a sinner is to convince of sin (John 16:8). And the more the Spirit works in a person, the

---

13. "The Absence of the Sense of Sin," *Banner of Sovereign Grace Truth* 6 (1998):262.

14. *Works of Jonathan Edwards,* ed. Edward Hickman (1834; reprint London: Banner of Truth Trust, 1974), 1:345.

more he is convicted of his unworthiness before God. The Spirit prompts such an awareness of God, that the sinner confesses along with Isaiah, "Woe is me! for I am undone; because I am a man of unclean lips...for mine eyes have seen the King, the LORD of hosts" (Isa. 6:5), and with Paul, "O wretched man that I am! who shall deliver me from the body of this death?" (Rom. 7:24). Does the lack of conviction of sin in much modern evangelism imply the absence of the Spirit whose convicting work is essential to salvation?

The church should take a fresh look at Scripture, the Puritans, and church history, which all show that God is pleased to work conviction through His Holy Spirit using men whose hearts He has broken and led to Christ, and who then go out to preach with hearts full of compassion for Christless sinners. In the words of John Willison, God raises up men "of large hearts," when He is going to save many people. We need today more biblical, holy, humble, prayerful, and heavenly ministers. We do not need stalwart polemicists and apologists so much as we need genuinely pious men of God who bring the atmosphere of heaven with them to the pulpit.[15]

When God is pleased to raise and use such men to bring others to a conviction of sin, there is something

---

15. Cf. Isaac Watts, "Rules for the Preacher's Conduct," in *The Christian Pastor's Manual*, ed. John Brown of Edinburgh (1826; reprint Ligonier, Pa.: Soli Deo Gloria, 1991), pp. 198-243; Gardiner Spring, *The Power of the Pulpit* (1848: Edinburgh: Banner of Truth Trust, 1986), pp. 137-66.

distinctive about their preaching. Such preaching purposefully aims to convict of sin, not just to alarm people, but to awaken them as sinners. Such preaching searches and "rips up the consciences" of men and women, as Perkins put it, boldly calling sinners to heartfelt repentance. And the Holy Spirit normally uses such preaching by bringing listeners to conviction of sin. When John the Baptist preached convictingly, people fled from the wrath to come (Matt. 3:1-12). When Peter preached convictingly on Pentecost, at least three thousand were pricked in their hearts (Acts 2:37).

By contrast, modern evangelism, dating in North America from Charles Finney, doesn't strive to bring sinners to repentance, partly because of its defective, Pelagian view of man and sin.[16] The Bible, however, abounds with teaching about sin as guilt, defilement, depravity, and corruption in the human heart. Reformed confessions of faith and Puritan theology are also clear and full of teaching on this subject. But many evangelists today say too little about sin, perhaps because they have little sense of sin themselves and because they believe that the first task of evangelism is to win people to Christ by addressing

---

16. See Packer, *A Quest for Godliness,* pp. 292-94; Iain Murray, *Revival and Revivalism: The Making and Marring of American Evangelicalism 1750-1858* (Edinburgh: Banner of Truth Trust, 1994), pp. 228ff., and *Pentecost—Today? The Biblical Basis for Understanding Revival* (Edinburgh: Banner of Truth Trust, 1998), pp. 33-53.

their "felt needs"—the things people think they need to hear about, rather than real spiritual needs related to sin.

Even among evangelists today who speak about the guilt of sin and man's need of forgiveness, they do not go far enough. They do not teach that "the natural man"—the non-Christian—is so dead in trespasses and sins (Eph. 2:1-3) that, left to himself, he is not able to seek God and His forgiveness (Rom. 3:9-18). They overlook verses such as Romans 8:7, "The carnal mind is enmity against God: for it is not subject to the law of God, neither indeed can be," and 1 Corinthians 2:14, "The natural man receiveth not the things of the Spirit of God: for they are foolishness unto him: neither can he know them, because they are spiritually discerned." Such texts are not relevant to evangelism, contemporary evangelists say, because "How can we speak of the sinner's depravity, then ask him to respond to the gospel?"[17]

The error of such thinking is the premise that any teaching on human sinfulness that denies a person's ability to respond is a hindrance to evangelism. They forget that only God can bring the dead to life and grant them faith to believe in His Son. They forget that He commands His servants to preach to valleys of dry, dead bones (Ezek. 37:1-14) and blesses the preaching of His Word by breathing life into those

17. Cf. Billy Graham, *The Holy Spirit: Activating God's Power in Your Life* (Waco, Tx.: Word, 1978).

bones and regenerating them by His Spirit. They forget that such an inward change of soul is generally accompanied with inward struggle and agony on account of sin.

The results, then, of the absence of a sense of sin in the modern pulpit reaps tragic fruit in the pew. Unconverted sinners are not warned of their sin and danger, and are seldom directed to the way of escape through Jesus Christ and Him crucified. Nominal professors are allowed to sleep on in self-complacency and carnal security. The believer is not urged to daily repentance and mortification of sin.[18]

Let us remember that the Puritan emphasis on conviction of sin is only the starting point for biblical, experiential, and practical evangelism. The ultimate aim of such preaching is to lead people, just as they are in all their sinfulness and need, to Jesus Christ, who alone can save them from eternal condemnation and present them holy before the Father.

18. Sinclair, "The Absence of the Sense of Sin," *Banner of Sovereign Grace Truth* 6 (1998):263.

◆

CHAPTER FIVE

Holistically Evangelistic

Puritan preaching was *holistically evangelistic.* The Puritans used all of Scripture to confront the whole man. They did not merely pressure the human will to respond on the basis of a few dozen texts that emphasize the volitional aspect of evangelism.

Modern evangelism stresses a decisional act of faith on the part of the sinner. It is convinced that the first aim of preaching is to call upon men to believe. It does not think the saving work of the Holy Spirit is necessary prior to faith. It holds that we believe in order to be born again, that faith precedes and effects regeneration. Faith, of course, is essential to salvation from beginning to end (e.g., Rom. 1:17; Heb. 11:6), and there is no time lapse between regeneration and the Spirit's implanting of saving faith in the heart of a sinner. Puritan evangelism, however, has a deeper and wider message to the unconverted.

Certainly the duty to respond to the gospel in faith is important, but so are other duties. There is the duty to repent, not just as a temporary feeling of sorrow, but as a full amendment of life. The Puritans preached that sinners are to "cease to do evil" (Isa. 1:16b), and to be holy as God is holy. They are to love God and His holy law with heart and mind and strength, and to let nothing stand in the way of obedience. They are to "strive to enter in at the strait gate" (Luke 13:24).[1]

Some church leaders would argue that such preaching leads to legalism. But such preaching is justified on this ground: In the work of conversion God does not normally begin with a conscious decision of faith but with conviction of sin and a sense of total helplessness to obey God's commands. Thus the Puritans preached the precepts of the law before they offered the promises of the gospel. They spoke about the obligations that lie upon sinners before showing the way of deliverance through faith in the blood of Christ.

Puritan evangelists preached the law before the gospel in much the same way Paul wrote the first three chapters of Romans. The apostle first explained the holiness of God and His law so that the mouths of sinners would be stopped and the whole world would be found guilty before God. The Puritans did not urge the wicked to turn from sin because they thought sinners could do so but because they believed that through such a confrontation with the demands of the law the Holy Spirit would bring sin-

---

1. Cf. Joel R. Beeke, *Knowing and Living the Christian Life* (Grand Rapids: Reformation Heritage Books, 1997), pp. 16-21.

ners to know their helplessness before God and their need for salvation.

The Puritans did not believe that such preaching prepared people for salvation by qualifying them to proceed to faith. That would have been legalistic, as some, including Spurgeon, have falsely charged several Puritans.[2] Rather, they believed that the gospel is meaningful only to sinners who recognize their sinfulness. Conviction—or the killing work of the law—is the way that leads to Christ, not a condition for receiving Christ. It is the normal way to faith, not the warrant of faith. The Puritans did recognize some exceptions, however. In *The Christian's Great Interest,* William Guthrie suggested four ways in which sinners are drawn to Christ:

1. Some, such as John the Baptist, are called from the womb;
2. Some, such as Zaccheus, are called as adults in a sovereign, gospel way;
3. Some, such as the thief on the cross, are graciously called at death's door; but
4. Most are called and prepared for Christ by the work of the law.

The first three ways of being drawn to Christ are exceptions; the fourth is the normal way of conviction. Guthrie then explains the difference between "the preparatory work of the law which leads to sal-

---

2. Packer, *A Quest for Godliness,* pp. 171-72.

vation and the temporary convictions of those who
relapse."[3]

The Puritans, then, were not afraid to use the law
of God as an instrument of evangelism. When God
is about to play the chord of grace in the soul, they
taught, he usually starts with the bass note of the
law. In order for man to come to Christ, he must first
come to an end of his own righteousness.[4] "They held
[that] the index of the soundness of a man's faith in
Christ is the genuineness of the self-despair from
which it springs," says Packer.[5]

This type of evangelism is clearly rooted in Scripture. John the Baptist preached repentance and
holiness (Matt. 3:1-2) before he preached, "Behold
the Lamb of God, which taketh away the sin of the
world" (John 1:29). Jesus began his ministry with
the same message. As Matthew 4:17 says, "From that
time Jesus began to preach, and to say, Repent: for
the kingdom of heaven is at hand." He continued
that theme with individuals such as Nicodemus, saying, "Ye must be born again" (John 3:7), and with the

---

3. Chapter 2, pp. 37-59.

4. Thomas Hooker, *The Soul's Preparation for Christ: Or, A
Treatise of Contrition, Wherein is discovered How God breaks
the heart, and wounds the Soul, in the conversion of a Sinner to
Himself* (1632; reprint Ames, Ia.: International Outreach, 1994),
pp. 121-55; Samuel Bolton, Nathaniel Vincent, and Thomas
Watson, *The Puritans on Conversion* (Pittsburgh: Soli Deo Gloria,
1990), pp. 107-113.

5. *A Quest for Godliness,* p. 170.

rich young ruler, confronting him first of all with the
commandments (Mark 10:19).

Law preaching is more than explaining the Ten
Commandments. It is preaching God's righteous
judgment and holy wrath against all ungodliness and
unrighteousness of men. It is preaching the attributes
of God. When Joseph Alleine wrote about the misery of the unconverted, for example, he showed how
several attributes of God—His holiness, faithfulness,
justice, and purity—condemn the sinner because
he has denied God's claims, spurned His laws, and
lies under His wrath and condemnation.[6] Alleine's
hope in preaching is that the Spirit of God will make
these truths so real to the sinner that he will become
receptive to the good news that the very God whose
attributes burn against him in righteous indignation
has provided a way of escape in Jesus Christ for just
such sinners as he.

The message of the Bible and the Puritans is:
The law has an evangelistic use.[7] Let man try to obey
the law for salvation. At first he will think he can do
it. Then he will learn that he cannot possibly be as
holy as the law demands. Wielded by the Spirit, the
law condemns him, pronounces a curse upon him,
and declares him liable to the wrath of God and the

---

6. *Alarm to the Unconverted,* pp. 85-88.

7. Joel R. Beeke and Ray B. Lanning, "Glad Obedience," in
Trust and Obey, ed. Don Kistler (Morgan, Pa.: Soli Deo Gloria,
1996), pp. 159-62.

torments of hell (Gal. 3:10). Finally, he will come to
the desperate realization that only God can save him
by changing his heart and giving him a new nature.
The Spirit brings him to the end of the law, Christ
Jesus, as the only righteousness acceptable with God
(Gal. 3:24).

So the old Puritan evangelists labored with the
law to convince sinners both of their need for salvation and the impossibility of accomplishing such
salvation themselves. Sinners who experience both
this necessity and impossibility cry out in anguish for
God to do for them what they cannot do for themselves. In this way sinners have room made in them
to receive the rich proclamation and application of
the gospel; the Spirit of God then enables them to
embrace Christ by faith.[8]

Modern evangelism differs from this in how it
persuades men to embrace the gospel. Puritans and
modern evangelists both use persuasive argument in
evangelism, but the content of those arguments differs.
Modern evangelists do not believe that the necessity
of holiness is a suitable subject for the unconverted,
so they do not present the gospel as a divine remedy
for corrupt and impotent sinners. Puritans, by contrast, believed that the best news in the world for

---

8. For a description of how faith embraces Christ, see Joel R.
Beeke, "The Relation of Faith to Justification," in *Justification by
Faith Alone,* ed. Don Kistler (Morgan, Pa.: Soli Deo Gloria, 1995),
pp. 68-78.

sinners who are truly convicted of sin is that deliverance from the power of sin is possible through faith in Christ. Such sinners need more than forgiveness or pardon; they want sin to be put to death in themselves forever. They want to live for the glory of God. They want to be holy as God is holy. They want to be conformed to the character of the Father, the image of the Son, and the mind of the Spirit.[9]

Joseph Alleine distinguished between true and false converts in this manner: "When [false converts] have as much as will save them, as they suppose, they look no farther, and so show themselves short of true grace, which always sets men aspiring to perfection (Phil. 3:13)."[10] An important mark of saving faith, then, is that a convert not only wants to be delivered from the corruption of sin, but that he also hungers and thirsts after righteousness and holiness.

Modern evangelism has lost sight of that motive. Holiness is treated as something separate from salvation. Thus the message that seeks to convince people to embrace Christ is generally an appeal to self-interest. It offers forgiveness with the assurance of heaven and the kind of happiness and satisfaction that is found in Christ, without mentioning fruits of sanctification such as self-denying humility and unconditional obedience. Thankfully, under such

---

9. Joel R. Beeke, *Holiness: God's Call to Sanctification* (Edinburgh: Banner of Truth Trust, 1994), p. 11.

10. *Alarm to the Unconverted,* p. 75.

defective preaching (by the mercy of God) some people are saved. But that doesn't make such preaching right. Such preaching often minimizes the difficulty of coming to Christ and overplays the temporal benefits of living life as a Christian. This type of preaching is an attempt to give men who have no conviction of sin an alternative reason to decide for Christ.

If being saved is presented as nothing more than professing faith in Christ, and if regeneration can happen without corresponding evidence of holy living, then the church will soon be filled with people who deceive themselves and others about their true spiritual condition. Those who have not been slain by the law will show little concern to keep the law once they believe they are Christians. And if they are taught that holiness isn't an essential part of being a Christian, they may live with that delusion the rest of the lives.

All of this leads us to conclude that the teaching of modern evangelism on the nature of faith and its relationship to regeneration fails the test of the Word of God. The Puritans taught that a "regeneration" which leaves men without the indwelling power of the Holy Spirit and without the practice of holy living is not what Scripture promises.[11] According to the Bible, a regenerate person is not simply changed in

---

11. William Whately, *The New Birth* (London, 1618); Stephen Charnock, "A Discourse of the Efficient of Regeneration," in *The Works of Stephen Charnock* (1865; reprint Edinburgh: Banner of Truth Trust, 1986), 3:166-306.

his religious opinions. A regenerate person is someone who has been given a new nature by the Holy Spirit. He is born of the Spirit to become spiritual (John 3:6). He has been recreated so all things are become new.[12] Such a person ceases to be self-centered and becomes God-centered. "They that are after the flesh do mind the things of the flesh; but they that are after the Spirit the things of the Spirit" (Rom. 8:5). The regenerate man loves God, loves holiness, loves the Bible, loves the godly, and loves the thought of going to heaven to commune with God and to leave sin behind forever.

Modern evangelism treats regeneration as the fruit of an initial act of faith in Christ. That is erroneous because, as the Puritans taught, a person may exercise a type of faith that isn't saving faith. John 2:23-25 says that many people believed in Jesus' name, but Jesus did not commit Himself to them because He knew what was in them. Scripture teaches that there are different kinds of faith. One kind of faith is an outward expression that is not backed by internal renewal. This is a kind of intellectual conviction that is little more than self-confidence in one's own opinions.

The discrepancies between Puritan and modern evangelism should prompt us to revert back to the older message where the whole of Scripture is addressed to the whole man.

---

12. "A Discourse on the Nature of Regeneration," ibid., 3:82-165.

CHAPTER SIX

———— ◆ ————

Studiously Symmetrical

Puritan preaching was *studiously symmetrical.*
There was in Puritan preaching both well-rounded-
ness and good balance. Puritan preaching achieved
this symmetry in four ways:

First, *Puritan preaching allowed Scripture to dic-
tate the emphasis for each message.* The Puritans
did not preach sermons that were a kind of balanc-
ing act between various doctrines. Rather, they let
the biblical text determine the content and emphasis
of each message. When Jonathan Edwards preached
on hell, for example, he didn't make a single refer-
ence to heaven. When he later preached on heaven,
he didn't include a word about hell.[1]

The Puritans preached a Bible text completely

---

1. Cf. *The Wrath of Almighty God: Jonathan Edwards on
God's Judgment against Sinners,* ed. Don Kistler (Morgan, Pa.:
Soli Deo Gloria, 1996); *The Works of Jonathan Edwards,* 2:617-
41; John H. Gerstner, *Jonathan Edwards on Heaven and Hell*
(Grand Rapids: Baker, 1980).

whatever its theme, so in time they would be sure
to address every major theme of Scripture and
every major doctrine of Reformed theology. Nothing was left unbalanced in the total range of their
frequent and lengthy sermons. In theology proper,
they proclaimed God's transcendence as well as His
immanence. In anthropology, they preached about
the image of God in its narrower as well as its wider
sense. In Christology, they exhibited Christ's state of
humiliation as well as exaltation. In soteriology, they
presented divine sovereignty and human responsibility as doctrines that do not need to be reconciled
by our finite minds, since as one preacher quipped,
"friends need no reconciliation." In ecclesiology, they
acknowledged the high calling of special offices (ministers, elders, and deacons) as well as the equally
high calling of the general office of all believers. In
eschatology, they declared both the glories of heaven
and the horrors of hell.

Second, *Puritan preaching instilled appreciation for
each scriptural doctrine.* The typical member of a
Puritan congregation could relish a sermon one week
on Genesis 19:17 ("Escape for thy life") for its warning notes on fleeing wickedness and following God,
and the next week savor a message on how difficult
it is to follow God unless God draws us to Himself
(John 6:44). Puritan pastors and people alike trea-
sured the full scope of God's biblical truth rather than
just their favorite passages or particular doctrines by
which they rated each sermon.

Third, *Puritan preaching allowed for a wide variety of sermon topics.* A carefully cultivated appreciation for all scriptural doctrine in turn allowed the Puritans to cover nearly every topic imaginable. For example, one volume of Puritan sermons includes the following messages:

- How May We Experience in Ourselves, and Evidence to Others, that Serious Godliness is more than a Fancy?

- What Are the Best Preservatives Against Melancholy and Overmuch Sorrow?

- How May We grow in the Knowledge of Christ?

- What Must We Do to Prevent and Cure Spiritual Pride?

- How May We Graciously Improve Those Doctrines and Providences That Transcend Our Understanding?

- What Distance Ought We to Keep, in Following the Strange Fashions of Apparel Which Come Up in the Days in Which We Live?

- How May We Best Know the Worth of the Soul?[2]

Modern evangelism, by contrast, is reductionistic—using only a few texts, expounding a limited

---

2. *Puritan Sermons 1659-1689: Being the Morning Exercises at Cripplegate,* ed. James Nichols (1682; reprint Wheaton, Ill.: Richard Owen Roberts, 1981), vol. 3.

range of themes, and bringing little if any doctrine to bear on the work of evangelism.

Fourth, *Puritan preaching was backed by right living*. Puritan preachers lived what they preached. For them, balanced doctrine was inseparable from balanced living. Puritan ministers were teaching prophets, interceding priests, and governing kings in their own homes as well as their congregations and society. They were men of private prayer, family worship, and public intercession. They were living illustrations of Robert Murray M'Cheyne's words: "A holy minister is an awful weapon in the hand of God.... A minister's life is the life of his ministry."[3] Or as John Boys put it: "He doth preach most, that doth live best."[4]

One of the glaring faults in modern evangelism is its lack of balance in word and deed. Modern evangelism presents a gospel that is so stripped of the demands of Christ's Lordship that it becomes cheap grace. And cheap grace produces cheap living.

We need to ask ourselves: Is our preaching, teaching, and evangelizing thoroughly scriptural, unashamedly doctrinal, experimentally practical, holistically evangelistic, and beautifully symmetrical?

---

3. *Memoir and Remains of Robert Murray M'Cheyne,* ed. Andrew A. Bonar (London: Banner of Truth Trust, 1966), p. 282.

4. *The Works of John Boys* (1629; reprint Morgan, Pa.: Soli Deo Gloria, 1997), p. 481.

The Method of
Puritan Evangelism

CHAPTER SEVEN

———————— ◆ ————————

Plain Preaching

Though evangelism differs to some degree from generation to generation according to gifts, culture, style, and language, the primary methods of Puritan evangelism—plain preaching and catechetical teaching—can teach us much about how to present the gospel to sinners.

The greatest teacher of the Puritan "plain style of preaching" was William Perkins. Perkins, often called the father of Puritanism, wrote that preaching "must bee plaine, perspicuous, and evident.... It is a by-word among us: *It was a very plaine Sermon:* And I say againe, *the plainer, the better.*"[1] Henry Smith, another great Puritan preacher, said, "To preach simply, is not to preach unlearnedly, nor confusedly, but plainly and perspicuously, that the simplest which

1. *The Works of Perkins,* 2:222. Cf. William Perkins, *The Art of Prophesying* (1606; revised ed., Edinburgh: Banner of Truth Trust, 1996), pp. 71-72; Charles H. George and Katherine George, *The Protestant Mind of the English Reformation 1570-1640* (Princeton: Princeton University Press, 1961), pp. 338-41.

doth hear, may understand what is taught, as if he did hear his name."[2] And Cotton Mather wrote succinctly in his eulogy for John Eliot, a great Puritan missionary to the Indians, that his "way of preaching was very plain; so that the very *lambs* might wade into his discourses on those texts and themes, wherein *elephants* might swim."[3]

The Puritans used the plain style of preaching because they were evangelistic to the core—they wanted to reach everyone, to preach so that all might know the way of salvation. This style of preaching, according to William Perkins, did three things:

---

2. *Works of Henry Smith,* 1:337. Cf. Leland Ryken, *Worldly Saints,* pp. 104-107.

3. *The Great Works of Christ in America: Magnalia Christi Americana,* Book III (1702; reprint London: Banner of Truth Trust, 1979), 1:547-48. For a bibliography of Eliot's sermons and writings, see Frederick Harling, "A Biography of John Eliot" (Ph.D. dissertation, Boston University, 1965), pp. 259-61. For additional material on Eliot, see John Wilson, *The Life of John Eliot* (New York: G. Land and P.P. Stanford, 1841); Martin More, *Memoir of Eliot* (Boston: Seth Goldsmith and Crocker & Brewster, 1842); Nehemiah Adams, *The Life of John Eliot* (Boston: Massachusetts School Society, 1847); Converse Francis, *Life of John Eliot, Apostle to the Indians* (Boston: Hilliard, Gray and Co., 1896); Ezra Hoyt Byington, "John Eliot, the Puritan Missionary to the Indians," in *Papers of the American Society of Church History* (New York: G. P. Putnam's Sons, 1897), 8:109-145; James de Normandie, "John Eliot, Apostle to the Indians," *Harvard Theological Review* 5 (1912):249-370; David Chamberlain, *Eliot of Massachusetts, Apostle to the Indians* (London: Independent Press, 1928); Rooy, *Missions in the Puritan Tradition,* pp. 156-241; Ola Elizabeth Winslow, *John Eliot, "Apostle to the Indians"* (Boston: Houghton Mifflin, 1968).

1. It gave the basic meaning of a text of Scripture in its context;
2. It expounded a few profitable points of doctrines gathered from the natural sense of the text;
3. It applied, in plain speech, the doctrines "rightly collected to the life and manners of men."[4]

The first part of a Puritan sermon was thus exegetical; the second, doctrinal and didactic; and the third, applicatory.[5] The third part, often called the "uses" of the text, was quite lengthy and applied Scripture in various ways to various listeners.[6] Perkins gave distinct directions on how to shape Scripture's applications to seven categories of listeners: ignorant and unteachable unbelievers; teachable but ignorant people; knowledgeable but unhumbled people; the humbled who lack assurance; believers; backsliders; and "a mingled people"—i.e., those who are a combination of several categories.[7] Puritan preachers addressed all seven types of people over a period of time, but not in each sermon. The Westminster Directory for Public Worship advises ministers not to pursue "every use" contained in the text being

---

4. *Works of Perkins,* 2:762. Cf. *The Art of Prophesying,* p. 79.

5. Perry Miller, *The New England Mind: The Seventeenth Century* (Cambridge: University Press, 1939), pp. 332-33.

6. Most Puritans preached from fifty to sixty minutes. They wrote out their sermons, particularly their application, in a much fuller way than they were actually preached.

7. *The Art of Prophesying,* pp. 56-63.

expounded. Each sermon did at least include directions to believers and unbelievers. The unbeliever
was usually called to examine how he was living and
what behavior needed changing, then admonished
to flee to Christ who alone could fulfil his needs. For
the believer, "uses" usually contained points of comfort, direction, and self-examination. The applicatory
part is "the life of preaching," wrote James Durham.
"Hence, preaching is called persuading, testifying,
beseeching, entreating, or requesting, exhorting."[8]

The studied, Word-centered plainness of Puritan
preaching was buttressed by Puritan hermeneutics.
J.I. Packer says that plain preaching helped the Puritans interpret the Bible literally and grammatically;
consistently and harmonistically; doctrinally and
theocentrically; christologically and evangelically;
experimentally and practically; and with a faithful
and realistic application.[9]

The Puritan plain style of preaching avoided all
that was not clear or "perspicuous" to an ordinary
listener. Since the minister was first and foremost
God's appointed interpreter of the Word, no
oratorical interest should ever be allowed to obscure
the gospel's truth and clarity. "A crucified style
best suits the preachers of a crucified Christ," John

---

8. *A Commentary upon the Book of the Revelation* (1660;
reprint Willow Street, PA: Old Paths Publications, 2000), p. 335.

9. *A Quest for Godliness,* chapter 6.

Flavel noted.[10] Lengthy quotations of the Fathers, the usage of Greek or Latin, and an embellished style were detested, for then we "do not paint Christ, but ourselves," said Perkins.[11] The heart of the true Christian, said Robert Bolton, "feeles itselfe more soundly comforted, and truly Christianized by one Sermon woven out of a feeling soule by the strength of meditation, supported by the true, naturall, and necessary sense of the Word of life, managed with the powerfull incomparable eloquence of Scripture...than with a world of generall [discourses] though they should be stuffed with the flower and quintessence of all the Arts, humanities, Philosophies."[12]

Three characteristics associated with Puritan plain preaching need to be recovered by today's preachers:

First, *Puritan preaching addressed the mind with clarity*. It addressed man as a rational creature. The Puritans loved and worshipped God with their minds. They viewed the mind as the palace of faith. They refused to set mind and heart against each other, but taught that knowledge was the soil in which the Spirit planted the seed of regeneration. "In conver-

10. *The Works of John Flavel* (1820; reprint London: Banner of Truth Trust, 1968), 6:572.

11. *Works of Perkins,* 2:222.

12. *The Workes of the Reverend, truly Pious, and Iudiciously learned Robert Bolton* (London: George Miller, 1641), 4:161.

sion, reason is elevated," John Preston wrote. And
Cotton Mather said, "Ignorance is the mother not of
devotion but of heresy." Puritans thus preached that
we need to *think* in order to be holy. They challenged
the idea that holiness is only a matter of emotions.

Puritan evangelists labored to show sinners the
unreasonableness of persisting in sin. They tore away
every excuse for remaining unregenerate, whether it
be an unbeliever's own inability and unwillingness, or
divine sovereignty and election. As John Owen told
his listeners, even election is no excuse for remaining in unbelief. "Election is first from God's side, but
it is known last from the believer's side," he said.[13]
Joseph Alleine added:

> You begin at the wrong end if you dispute about
> your election. Prove your conversion and then
> never doubt your election.... Whatever God's
> purposes be, which are secret, His promises are
> plain. How desperately do rebels argue, "If I am
> elected I shall be saved, do what I will. If not, I
> shall be damned, do what I can." Perverse sinner,
> will you begin where you should end? Is not the
> word before you? What saith it? *"Repent and be
> converted that your sins may be blotted out." "If
> you mortify the deeds of the body you shall live."
> "Believe and be saved"* (Acts 3:19; Rom. 8:13; Acts
> 16:31). What can be plainer? Do not stand still
> disputing about your election, but set to repent-

---

13. Cf. *Works of Owen,* 3:595-604. See also Christopher Love, *A
Treatise of Effectual Calling and Election* (1658; reprint Morgan,
Pa.: Soli Deo Gloria, 1998).

ing and believing. Cry to God for converting grace.
Revealed things belong to you; in these busy
yourself.[14]

So the Puritans reasoned with sinners through
plain preaching, using biblical logic to persuade each
listener that it was foolish not to seek and serve God
because of the value and purpose of life, and the cer-
tainty of death and eternity.

God gave us minds for a reason, the Puritans
taught. It is crucial that we become like Christ in the
way we think. Our minds must be enlightened by faith
and disciplined by the Word, then put into God's service in the world. We ought to be challenged by the
Puritans to use our intellect to further God's kingdom
through scriptural evangelism. Without clear thinking, we will never be able to evangelize and counter
the culture in which we live, work, and minister. We
will become empty in ourselves, non-productive, and
narcissistic, lacking a developing interior life.

The Puritans preached that a flabby mind is
no badge of honor. They understood that a mind-
less Christianity will foster a spineless Christianity.
An anti-intellectualistic gospel will spawn an irrel-
evant gospel that doesn't go beyond "felt needs."
That's what is happening in our churches today. We
have lost our Christian mind, and for the most part
we don't see the necessity of recovering it. We do
not understand that where there is little difference

---

14. *Alarm to the Unconverted,* p. 30.

between the Christian and non-Christian in what we think and believe, there will soon be little difference in how we live.

Second, *Puritan preaching confronted the conscience pointedly.* The Puritans worked hard on the consciences of sinners as the "light of nature" in them. Plain preaching named specific sins, then asked questions to press home the guilt of those sins upon the consciences of men, women, and children. As one Puritan wrote, "We must go with the stick of divine truth and beat every bush behind which a sinner hides, until like Adam who hid, he stands before God in his nakedness." They believed that was necessary because until the sinner gets out from behind that bush, he will never cry to be clothed in the righteousness of Christ.

So the Puritans preached *urgently*, believing that many of their listeners were still on their way to hell. They preached *directly*, confronting their hearers with law and gospel, with death in Adam and life in Christ. They preached *specifically*, taking seriously Christ's command "that repentance and remission of sins should be preached in his name" (Luke 24:47).

Today, modern evangelism is, for the most part, afraid to confront the conscience pointedly. We need to learn from the Puritans who were solemnly persuaded as they evangelized that the friend who loves you most, will tell you the most truth about yourself. Like Paul and the Puritans, we need to testify earnestly and with tears, of the need for "repentance toward God, and faith toward our Lord Jesus Christ" (Acts 20:21).

Third, *Puritan preaching wooed the heart passionately.* It was affectionate, zealous, and optimistic. It is unusual today to find a ministry which both feeds the mind with solid biblical substance and moves the heart with affectionate warmth, but this combination was commonplace with the Puritans. They did not just reason with the mind and confront the conscience; they appealed to the heart. They preached out of love for God's Word, love for the glory of God, and love for the soul of every listener. They preached with warm gratitude of the Christ who had saved them and made their lives a sacrifice of praise. They set forth Christ in His loveliness, hoping to make the unsaved jealous of what the believer has in Christ.

The Puritans used every weapon they could— compelling preaching, personal pleading, earnest praying, biblical reasoning, joyful living—to turn sinners from the road of destruction to God. And they believed that God would use their preaching as a weapon to conquer and a power to convert sinners. They believed that God exalted Christ "with his right hand to be a Prince and a Saviour, for to give repentance to Israel, and forgiveness of sins" (Acts 5:31). They knew from Scripture and by experience that only an omnipotent Christ can arrest a dead sinner wedded to his sinful lusts, divorce him from the primary love of his heart, make him willing to forsake his bosom sin, and turn him to God with full resolve to obey and honor Him and make Him his end and goal. They preached knowing that Christ, not our old Adamic nature, was sufficient for these things. "Preaching, therefore, ought not to be dead, but alive and effective so that an unbeliever coming into the congregation of believers should be affected and, as it were, transfixed by the very hearing of the word so that he might give glory to God," wrote William Ames.[15]

---

15. *The Marrow of Theology,* p. 194.

———— ◆ ————

CHAPTER EIGHT

Catechetical Evangelism

Like the Reformers, the Puritans were catechists. They believed that pulpit messages should be reinforced by personalized ministry through catechesis—the instruction in the doctrines of Scripture using catechisms. Puritan catechizing was evangelistic in several ways:

First, scores of Puritans reached out evangelistically to children and young people by writing catechism books that explained fundamental Christian doctrines via questions and answers supported by Scripture.[1] For example, John Cotton titled his catechism, *Milk*

---

1. See George Edward Brown, "Catechists and Catechisms of Early New England" (D.R.E. dissertation, Boston University, 1934); R.M.E. Paterson, "A Study in Catechisms of the Reformation and Post-Reformation Period" (M.A. thesis, Durham University, 1981); P. Hutchinson, "Religious Change: The Case of the English Catechism, 1560-1640" (Ph.D. dissertation, Stanford University, 1984); Ian Green, *The Christian's ABC: Catechisms and Catechizing in England c. 1530-1740* (Oxford: Clarendon Press, 1996).

for Babes, drawn out of the Breasts of both Testaments.[2] Other Puritans included in the titles of their catechisms such expressions as "the main and fundamental points," "the sum of the Christian religion," the "several heads" or "first principles" of religion, and "the ABC of Christianity." Ian Green shows the high level of continuity that exists in Puritan catechism books in their recurring formulae and topics such as the Apostles' Creed, the Ten Commandments, the Lord's Prayer, and the sacraments. He goes on to suggest that there really was no substantial discrepancy even between the simple message of many elementary works and the more demanding content of more sophisticated catechisms.[3] At various levels in the church as well as in the homes of their parishioners, Puritan ministers taught rising generations both from the Bible and from their catechisms. Their goals were to explain the fundamental teachings of the Bible, to help young people commit the Bible to memory, to make sermons and the sacraments more understandable, to prepare covenant children for confession of faith, to teach them how to defend their faith against error, and to help parents teach their own children.[4]

---

2. London, 1646.

3. *The Christian's ABC,* pp. 557-70.

4. Cf. W.G.T. Shedd, *Homiletics and Pastoral Theology* (1867; reprint London: Banner of Truth Trust, 1965), pp. 356-75.

Second, catechizing was evangelistic in relation to both sacraments. When the Westminster Larger Catechism speaks of "improving" one's baptism, it refers to a task of lifelong instruction in which catechisms such as the Shorter Catechism play a decisive role.[5] William Perkins said that the ignorant should memorize his catechism, *The Foundation of Christian Religion,* so they would be "fit to receive the Lord's Supper with comfort." And William Hopkinson wrote in the preface to *A Preparation into the Waie of Life,* that he labored to lead his catechumens "into the right use of the Lord's Supper, a special confirmation of God's promises in Christ."[6]

The more their public efforts to purify the church were crushed, the more the Puritans turned to the home as a bastion for religious instruction and influence. They wrote books on family worship and the "godly order of family government." Robert Openshawe prefaced his catechism with an appeal "to those who were wont to ask how you should spend the long winter evenings, [to] turn to singing of psalms and

---

5. The Westminster Assembly desired to establish one catechism and one confession of faith for both England and Scotland, but a large number of catechisms continued to be written after the Westminster standards were drafted (J. Lewis Wilson, "Catechisms, and Their Use Among the Puritans," in *One Steadfast High Intent* [London: Puritan and Reformed Studies Conference, 1966], pp. 41-42).

6. *A Preparation into the Waie of Life, with a Direction into the righte use of the Lordes Supper* (London, 1583), sig. A.3.

teaching your household and praying with them."[7] By
the time of the Westminster Assembly in the 1640s,
the Puritans considered the lack of family worship to
be an evidence of an unconverted life.[8]

Third, catechizing was a follow-up to sermons and a
way to reach neighbors with the gospel. Joseph Alleine reportedly followed up his work on Sunday five
days a week by catechizing church members as well as
reaching out with the gospel to people he met on the
streets.[9] Richard Baxter, whose vision for catechizing
is expounded in *The Reformed Pastor,* said that he
came to the painful conclusion that "some ignorant
persons, who have been so long unprofitable hearers,
have got more knowledge and remorse of conscience
in half an hour's close disclosure, than they did from
ten years' public preaching."[10] Baxter thus invited
people in his home every Thursday evening to dis-
cuss and pray for blessing upon the sermons of the
previous Sabbath.

---

7. *Short Questions and Answeares* (London, 1580), p. A.4.

8. Wilson, "Catechisms, and Their Use Among the Puritans,"
pp. 38-39.

9. C. Stanford, *Joseph Alleine: His Companions and Times*
(London, 1861).

10. Richard Baxter, *Gidlas Salvianus: The Reformed Pastor:
Shewing the Nature of the Pastoral Work* (1656; reprint New
York: Robert Carter, 1860), pp. 341-468.

Fourth, catechizing was evangelistic for purposes of examining people's spiritual condition, and for encouraging and admonishing them to flee to Christ. Baxter and his two assistants spent two full days each week catechizing parishioners in their homes. In addition to that, on Monday and Tuesday afternoons and evenings he catechized each of his seven family members for an hour per week. Those visits involved patiently teaching, gently examining, and carefully leading family and church members to Christ through the Scriptures. Packer concludes: "To upgrade the practice of personal catechising from a preliminary discipline for children to a permanent ingredient in evangelism and pastoral care for all ages was Baxter's main contribution to the development of Puritan ideals for the ministry."[11]

Puritan churches and schools considered catechism instruction so important that some even offered official catechists. At Cambridge University, William Perkins served as catechist at Christ's College and John Preston at Emanuel College. The Puritan ideal, according to Thomas Gataker, was that a school is a "little church" and its teachers "private catechists."[12]

Puritan evangelism, carried on by preaching, pastoral admonition, and catechizing, took time and

---

11. *A Quest for Godliness,* p. 305.

12. *David's Instructor* (London, 1620), p. 18; see also B. Simon, "Leicestershire Schools 1635-40," *British Journal of Educational Studies* (Nov. 1954):47-51.

skill.[13] The Puritans were not looking for quick and easy conversions; they were committed to building up lifelong believers whose hearts, minds, wills, and affections were won to the service of Christ.[14] Some pastors were more gifted than others at catechizing, but all were called to be evangelistic catechists.

The hard work of the Puritan catechist was greatly rewarded. Richard Greenham claimed that catechism teaching built up the Reformed church and did serious damage to Roman Catholicism.[15] When Baxter was installed at Kidderminster in Worcestershire, perhaps one family in each street honored God in family worship; at the end of his ministry there, there were streets where every family did so. He could say that of the six hundred converts that were brought to faith under his preaching, he could not name one that had backslidden to the ways of the world. How vastly different was that result compared to the results of today's evangelists who press for mass conversions, then turn over the hard work of follow-up to others!

---

13. Thomas Boston, *The Art of Manfishing: A Puritan's View of Evangelism,* intro. J.I. Packer (reprint Fearn, Ross-shire: Christian Focus, 1998), pp. 14-15.

14. Thomas Hooker, *The Poor Doubting Christian Drawn to Christ* (1635; reprint Worthington, Pa.: Maranatha, 1977).

15. *A Short Forme of Catechising* (London: Richard Bradocke, 1599).

The Inward Disposition
of the Puritan Evangelist

———————◆———————

CHAPTER NINE

Dependency on the Holy Spirit

The Puritan evangelist brought to his work a unique inward disposition or frame of mind and soul. Commitment to godliness lay at the heart of the Puritan vision. Thomas Brooks wrote, "A preacher's life should be a commentary upon his doctrine; his practice should be the counterpane [counterpart] of his sermons. Heavenly doctrines should always be adorned with a heavenly life."

Preachers are the glass [the mirror],
the school, the book,
Where people's eyes do learn, do read, do look.[1]

The Puritan evangelist had a heart to serve God; devotion to and care for the people of God and the unsaved; devotion to the Scriptures and ability to preach them; a sense of dependency on the Holy Spirit coupled with a life of prayerfulness. These last two qualities in particular are lacking in modern

———————

1. *Works of Thomas Brooks,* 4:24.

evangelism and need to be addressed in our concluding chapters.

First, *the Puritans showed a profound dependence
upon the Holy Spirit* in everything they said and did.
They felt keenly their inability to bring anyone to
Christ as well as the magnitude of conversion. "God
never laid it upon thee to convert those he sends thee
to. No; to publish the gospel is thy duty," William
Gurnall said to ministers.[2] And Richard Baxter wrote,
"Conversion is another kind of work than most are
aware of. It is not a small matter to bring an earthly
mind to heaven and to show man the amiable excel-
lencies of God, to be taken up in such love to him
that can never be quenched; to make him flee for ref-
uge to Christ and thankfully embrace him as the life
of his soul; to have the very drift and bent of his life
change so that a man renounces that which he took
for his happiness, and places his happiness where he
never did before."[3]

The Puritans were convinced that both preacher
and listener are totally dependent on the work of the
Spirit to effect regeneration and conversion when,
how, and in whom He will.[4] The Spirit brings God's

---

2. *The Christian in Complete Armour* (1662; reprint London:
Banner of Truth Trust, 1964), p. 574 (second pagination).

3. Cf. Richard Baxter, *Reformed Pastor,* abridged (1862;
reprint London: Banner of Truth Trust, 1974), pp. 94-96, 114-16.

4. Packer, *A Quest for Godliness,* pp. 296-99.

presence into human hearts. He persuades sinners
to seek salvation, renews corrupt wills, and makes
scriptural truths take root in stony hearts. As Thomas
Watson wrote, "Ministers knock at the door of men's
hearts, the Spirit comes with a key and opens the
door."[5] And Joseph Alleine said: "Never think you
can convert yourself. If ever you would be savingly
converted, you must despair of doing it in your own
strength. It is a resurrection from the dead (Eph.
2:1), a new creation (Gal. 6:15; Eph. 2:10), a work of
absolute omnipotence (Eph. 1:19)."[6]

Modern evangelists need to be persuaded that
the Spirit's regenerating action, as John Owen wrote,
is "infallible, victorious, irresistible, and always
efficacious"; it "removeth all obstacles, overcomes
all oppositions, and infallibly produces the effect
intended."[7] All modes of action which imply another
doctrine are unbiblical. As Packer writes: "All devices
for exerting psychological pressure in order to precip-
itate 'decisions' must be eschewed, as being in truth
presumptuous attempts to intrude into the prov-
ince of the Holy Ghost." Such pressures may even
be harmful, he goes on to say, for while they "may
produce the outward form of 'decision,' they cannot
bring about regeneration and a change of heart, and
when the 'decisions' wear off those who registered

---

5. *A Body of Divinity,* p. 154.

6. *An Alarm to the Unconverted,* pp. 26-27.

7. *Works,* 3:317ff.

them will be found 'gospel-hardened' and antagonis-
tic." Packer concludes in a Puritan vein: "Evangelism
must rather be conceived as a long-term enterprise
of patient teaching and instruction, in which God's
servants seek simply to be faithful in delivering the
gospel message and applying it to human lives, and
leave it to God's Spirit to draw men to faith through
this message in his own way and at his own speed."[8]

---

8. *A Quest for Godliness,* pp. 163-64.

CHAPTER TEN

Men of Prayer

Finally, *the Puritans saturated all their evangelistic efforts in prayer.* They were "men of the closet" first of all. They were great preachers only because they were also great petitioners who wrestled with God for divine blessing upon their preaching. Richard Baxter said, "Prayer must carry on our work as well as preaching; he preacheth not heartily to his people, that prayeth not earnestly for them. If we prevail not with God to give them faith and repentance, we shall never prevail with them to believe and repent."[1] And Robert Traill wrote, "Some ministers of meaner gifts and parts are more successful than some that are far above them in abilities; not because they preach better, so much as because they pray more. Many good sermons are lost for lack of much prayer in study."[2]

The well-known story of Puritan-minded Robert Murray M'Cheyne illustrates best what Traill means.

---

1. *The Reformed Pastor,* p. 123.
2. *Works of Robert Traill,* 1:246.

An old sexton in M'Cheyne's church noticed the awe on the face of a visitor and invited him into his study. "Tell me," said the visitor, "having sat under this godly man's ministry, what is the secret of his success?"

The sexton told the visitor to sit at M'Cheyne's desk. Then he asked the man to put his hands on the desk. Then to put his face in his hands and weep. Next the two men walked into the church sanctuary and ascended to the pulpit. "Lean over the pulpit," the sexton said. "Now stretch out your hands and weep." "Now you know the secret of M'Cheyne's ministry."[3]

The church today desperately needs such preachers whose private prayers season their pulpit messages. The Puritan pastors jealously guarded their personal devotional time. They set their priorities on spiritual, eternal realities. They knew that if they ceased to watch and pray constantly they would be courting spiritual disaster. Faithful, steadfast, and sincere, they were God-fearing men who continually examined themselves and were painfully aware, as John Flavel said, "that a man may be *objectively* a *spiritual [man],* and all the while *subjectively* a *carnal* man."[4] They believed, as John Owen noted: "No man preacheth that sermon well that doth not first preach it to his own heart.... If the word do not dwell

---

3. Cf. John Flavel, "The Character of a True Evangelical Pastor," in *Works of Flavel,* 6:564-85.

4. Ibid., p. 568.

with power *in* us, it will not pass with power *from* us."[5] Unlike many modern evangelists, the quality of their spiritual life was uniformly high.[6]

Concluding Application

Let us seriously ask ourselves: Are we, like the Puritans, thirsting to glorify the triune God? Are we motivated by biblical truth and biblical fire? Do we share the Puritan view of the vital necessity of conversion? It is not enough just to read the Puritans. A stirring of interest in the Puritans is not the same thing as a revival of Puritanism. We need the inward disposition of the Puritans toward evangelism. We need in our hearts, lives, and churches the authentic, biblical, intelligent piety the Puritans showed.

Let us challenge one another! Who among us will live godly in Christ Jesus like the Puritans? Who will go beyond studying their writings, discussing their ideas, recalling their achievements, and berating their failures? Who will practice the degree of obedience to God's Word for which they strove? Will we serve God as they served Him? "Thus saith the LORD, Stand ye in the ways, and see, and ask for the old

---

5. *Works,* 9:455, 16:76.

6. See Benjamin Brook, *The Lives of the Puritans,* 3 vols. (1813; reprint Pittsburgh: Soli Deo Gloria, 1994); Joel R. Beeke and Randall J. Pederson, *Meet the Puritans* (Grand Rapids: Reformation Heritage Books, 2006); William Barker, *Puritan Profiles* (Fearn, Ross-shire: Christian Focus, 1996).

paths, where is the good way, and walk therein, and ye shall find rest for your souls" (Jer. 6:16).

We must ourselves be conquered by the great and mighty truths of God. The time is short. Soon we shall pray our last prayer, read Scripture for the last time, preach our last sermon, and witness to our last friend. Then the only thing that will matter will be the gospel. Surely on our deathbed a question uppermost in our minds will be: What kind of an evangelist have I been? Scripture tells us: "He that winneth souls is wise" (Prov. 11:30). "And they that be wise shall shine as the brightness of the firmament; and they that turn many to righteousness as the stars for ever and ever" (Dan. 12:3).

Also available from
Reformation Heritage Books

MEET THE PURITANS
With A Guide to Modern Reprints
by Joel R. Beeke and Randall J. Pederson

Meet the Puritans provides a bio-graphical and theological introduction to the Puritans whose works have been reprinted in the last fifty years, and also gives helpful summaries and insightful analyses of those reprinted works. It contains nearly 150 bio-graphical entries, and nearly 700 summaries of reprinted works.

978-1-60178-000-3   Hardback, 932 pages

LOVING CHRIST AND FLEEING TEMPTATION
by Andrew Gray

Loving Christ and Fleeing Temptation was first published in 1765 as *Select Sermons* from handwritten manuscripts. The present edition is freshly typeset and edited from the 1792 edition. These fifty sermons show why Gray was so popular as a preacher. They make doc-trine intelligible and practical. Gray's profound insights, poignant statements, and succinct summaries on the pre-ciousness of Christ, resisting the devil, spiritual pride, temptation, prayer, and many other truths are priceless.

978-1-60178-018-8   Hardback, 640 pages